THE BOOK AND CD ▼ THAT WORK TOGETHER

AZTECS

CHANHASSEN, MINNESOTA

Two-Can Publishing
An imprint of Creative Publishing international, Inc.
18705 Lake Drive East
Chanhassen, MN 55317
1-800-328-3895
www.two-canpublishing.com

Created by
act-two

CD
Creative Director: Jason Page
Programming Director: Paul Steven
Art Director: Sarah Evans
Designer: James Evans
Editor: Lyndall Thomas
Programmer: Colette McFadden
Consultant: Elizabeth Baquedano
Illustrators: James Jarvis, Jeffrey Lewis
Jon Stuart, Carlo Tartaglia
Production Director: Lorraine Estelle
Production Assistant: Bob Bridle
Project manager: Joya Bart-Plange

Book
Creative Director: Jason Page
Editor: Lyndall Thomas
Designer: Michele Egar
Consultant: Penny Bateman
Production Director: Lorraine Estelle
Production Assistant: Bob Bridle
Project Manager: Joya Bart-Plange

ISBN 1-58728-450-2

Photographic Credits: Werner Forman: front cover, pp12-16, pp18-19, p20 c, p21, p22,
pp 24-25, p26, p 34 cl, p47; Toby Maudsley: p19 b, p20 tr; Ronald Sheridan: p12 bl, p17, p34 tr
Illustrations: Harry Clow: pp10-11, p13, p17, p18, pp20-21, pp22-23, p24, p27, p28, p48;
Maxine Hamil: pp29-33; Linden Artists: p8, p9, p35

2 3 4 5 6 08 07 06 05 04

Printed in China

INTERFACT

THE BOOK AND CD THAT WORK TOGETHER

INTERFACT will have you hooked in minutes – and that's a fact!

The disk is packed with interactive activities, puzzles, quizzes, and games that are fun to do and packed with interesting facts.

Answer as many quiz questions as you can to win balls you can use on the tlachtli court.

Open the book and discover more fascinating information highlighted with lots of full-color illustrations and photographs.

Use the controls to adjust the power and angle of your hit

Read up on what the Aztecs ate, then do some cooking of your own!

To get the most out of **INTERFACT**, use the book and disk together. Look out for the special signs, called Disk Links and Bookmarks. To find out more, turn to page 43.

23

BOOKMARK

DISK LINK
Try an Aztec board game on screen when you Play Patolli!

Once you've launched **INTERFACT**, you'll never look back.

LOAD UP!
Go to **page 40** to find out how to load your disk and click into action.

What's on the disk

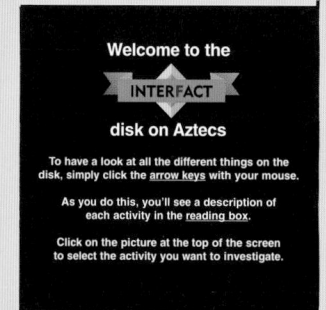

Welcome to the

INTERFACT

disk on Aztecs

To have a look at all the different things on the disk, simply click the arrow keys with your mouse.

As you do this, you'll see a description of each activity in the reading box.

Click on the picture at the top of the screen to select the activity you want to investigate.

HELP SCREEN

Learn how to use the disk in no time at all.

Get to grips with the controls and find out how to use:

- arrow keys
- text boxes
- "hot" words

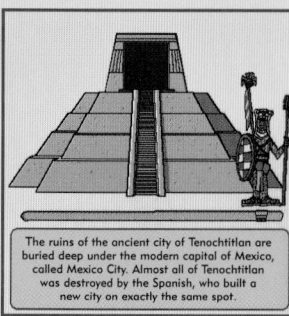

The ruins of the ancient city of Tenochtitlan are buried deep under the modern capital of Mexico, called Mexico City. Almost all of Tenochtitlan was destroyed by the Spanish, who built a new city on exactly the same spot.

TIME WARP

Take a trip through time and learn about ancient Mexico.

Discover how the Aztec civilisation began. Learn about the leaders who made the Aztec Empire powerful, and then find out how the Spanish invasion destroyed the Aztec way of life.

TLACHTLI CHALLENGE

Get ready to play the sacred Aztec ball game!

Answer quiz questions about the Aztecs and earn balls for use on the tlachtli court. Shoot for the hoop and see how many points you can score.

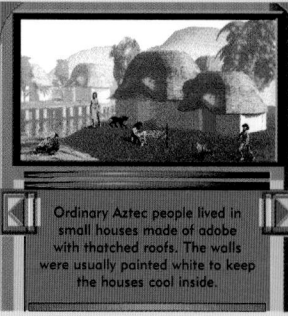

Ordinary Aztec people lived in small houses made of adobe with thatched roofs. The walls were usually painted white to keep the houses cool inside.

AZTEC EXPLORER

Take a scenic tour through the ancient Aztec lands!

Explore Tenochtitlan, the mighty city at the center of the Aztec Empire! Take a close-up look at an Aztec farm, or get the inside story on the temple precinct.

THE GREAT SPEAKER

Get the answers to all your questions about the Aztecs.

If there is something you want to know about the Aztecs, just ask the great speaker. He will answer questions from the crowd and will tell you all about life in Aztec times.

FOR SALE

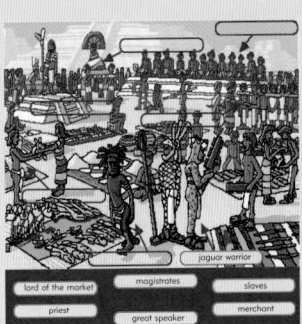

Investigate the amazing Aztec market at Tlatelolco.

See if you can figure out who is who in this busy market scene. Once you've put all the name tags in the right positions, go exploring with your mouse and find out what's going on.

SURVIVAL ADVENTURE

Put yourself to the test in an interactive adventure story.

Would you like to live in Aztec times? Travel back through history and find out! You'll need to use all your knowledge of the Aztecs to survive.

PLAY PATOLLI

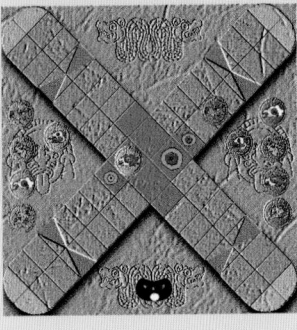

Learn how to play a traditional Aztec game.

Challenge a friend to a game of patolli, the Aztecs' favorite board game. Place your bets, throw the beans, and decide how to make your move!

What's in the book

*All words in the text that appear in **bold** can be found in the glossary*

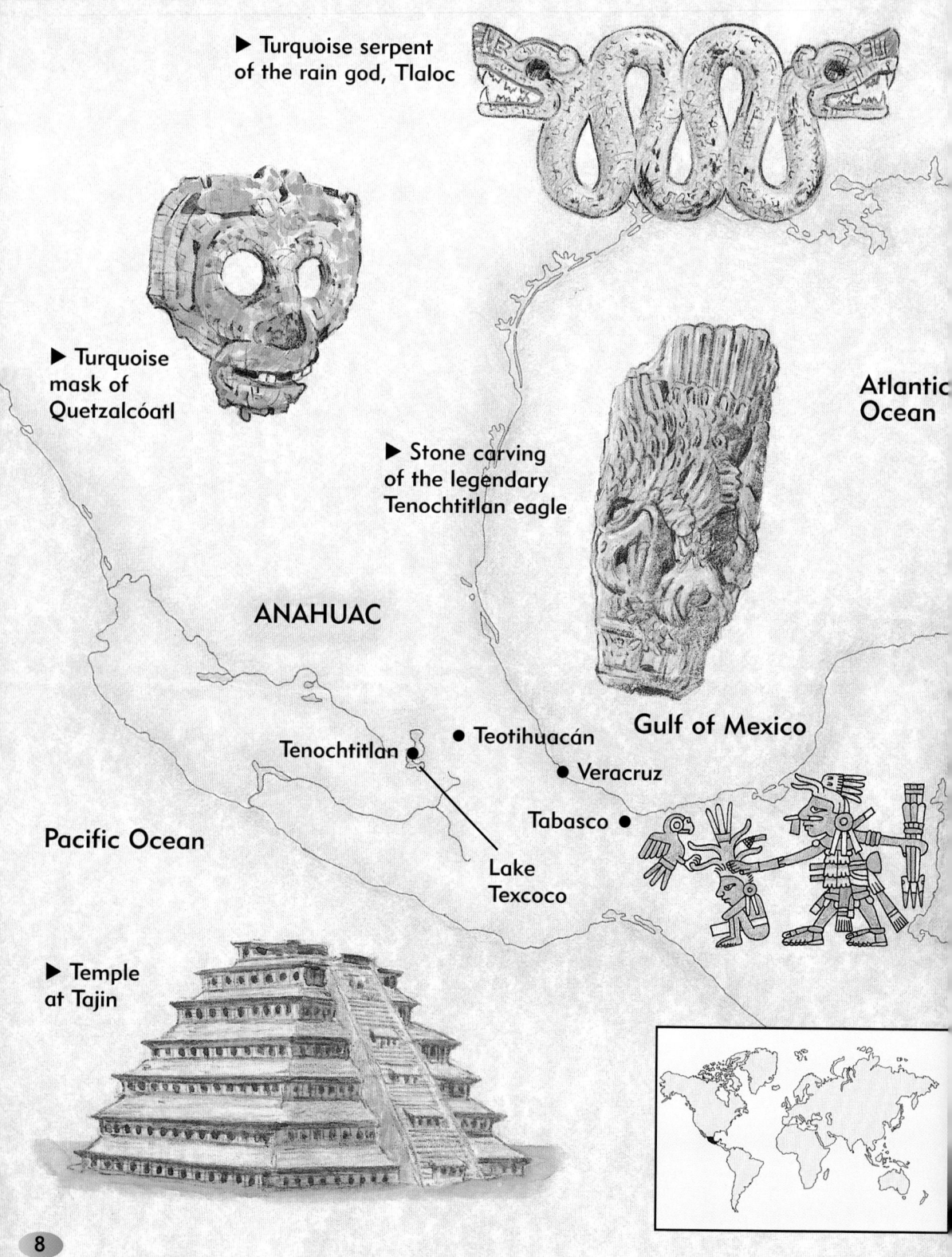

► Turquoise serpent of the rain god, Tlaloc

► Turquoise mask of Quetzalcóatl

► Stone carving of the legendary Tenochtitlan eagle

Atlantic Ocean

ANAHUAC

Gulf of Mexico

Tenochtitlan •

• Teotihuacán

• Veracruz

Tabasco •

Pacific Ocean

Lake Texcoco

► Temple at Tajin

8

The Aztec world

About 500 years ago, a group of people known as the Aztecs ruled the region we now call Mexico. They called their land **Anahuac**, which means *the land on the edge of the waters*.

The Aztecs were powerful warriors. They built a huge **empire** by attacking and conquering neighboring peoples.

▼ Every Aztec town had a busy marketplace.

Tenochtitlan

The capital of the Aztec Empire was called Tenochtitlan. It was built in the middle of a large lake on a **plateau** high in the mountains.

Tenochtitlan had a population of up to 300,000 people. This made it one of the largest cities in the world at that time.

Tenochtitlan was divided into four districts. The different parts of the city were connected by canals. The most important area was the temple precinct (shown below). Ordinary people lived in neighborhoods around the center of the city or in towns on the edge of the lake.

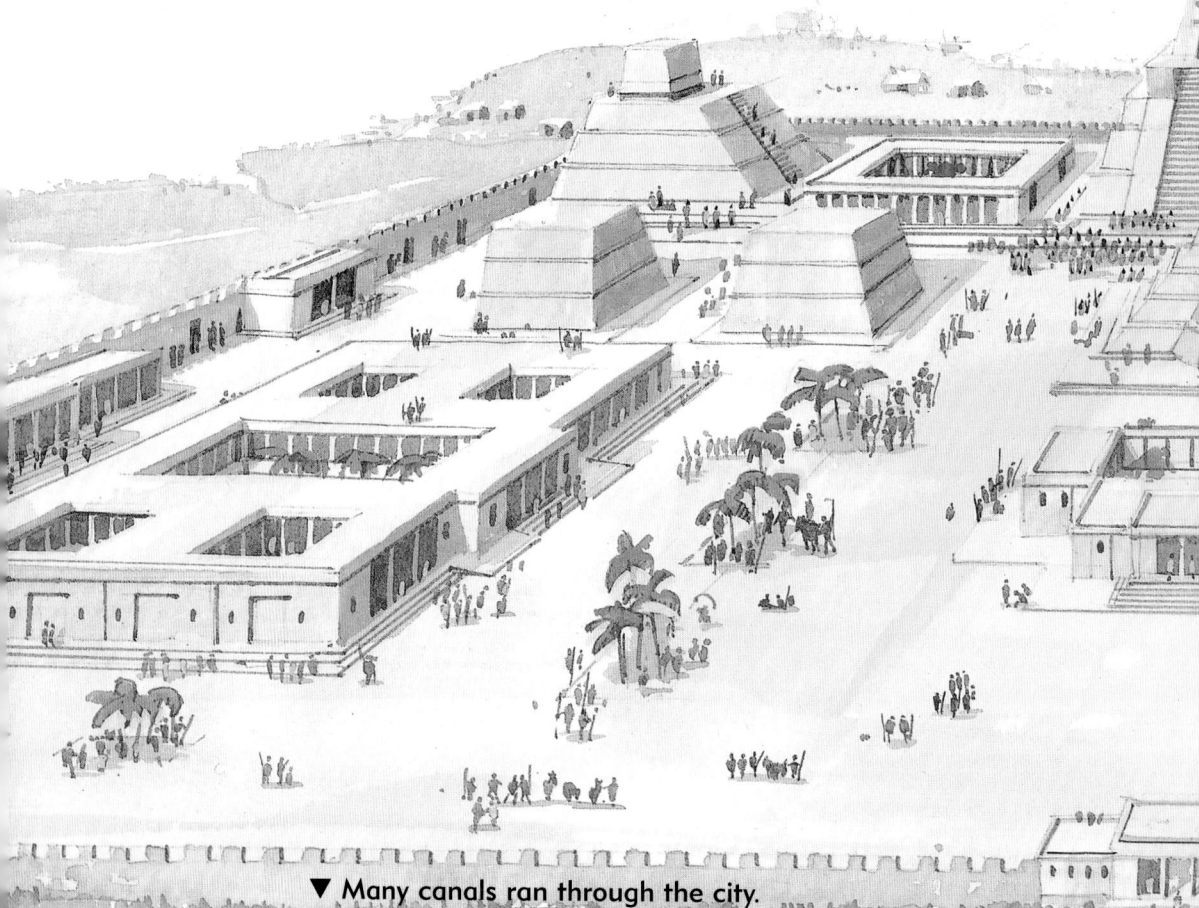

▼ Many canals ran through the city. The Aztecs did not have horses or vehicles with wheels. They carried everything by boat or on their backs.

▼ In the middle of Tenochtitlan was the temple precinct. The Aztecs worshiped their gods and performed human **sacrifices** there. The largest temple was about 295 feet (90 m) tall, and more than 100 steps led up to the top.

DISK LINK
Would you like a closer look at Tenochtitlan? Then venture forth in the Aztec Explorer.

▼ Tenochtitlan was built on an island in Lake Texcoco. The land there was damp and marshy.

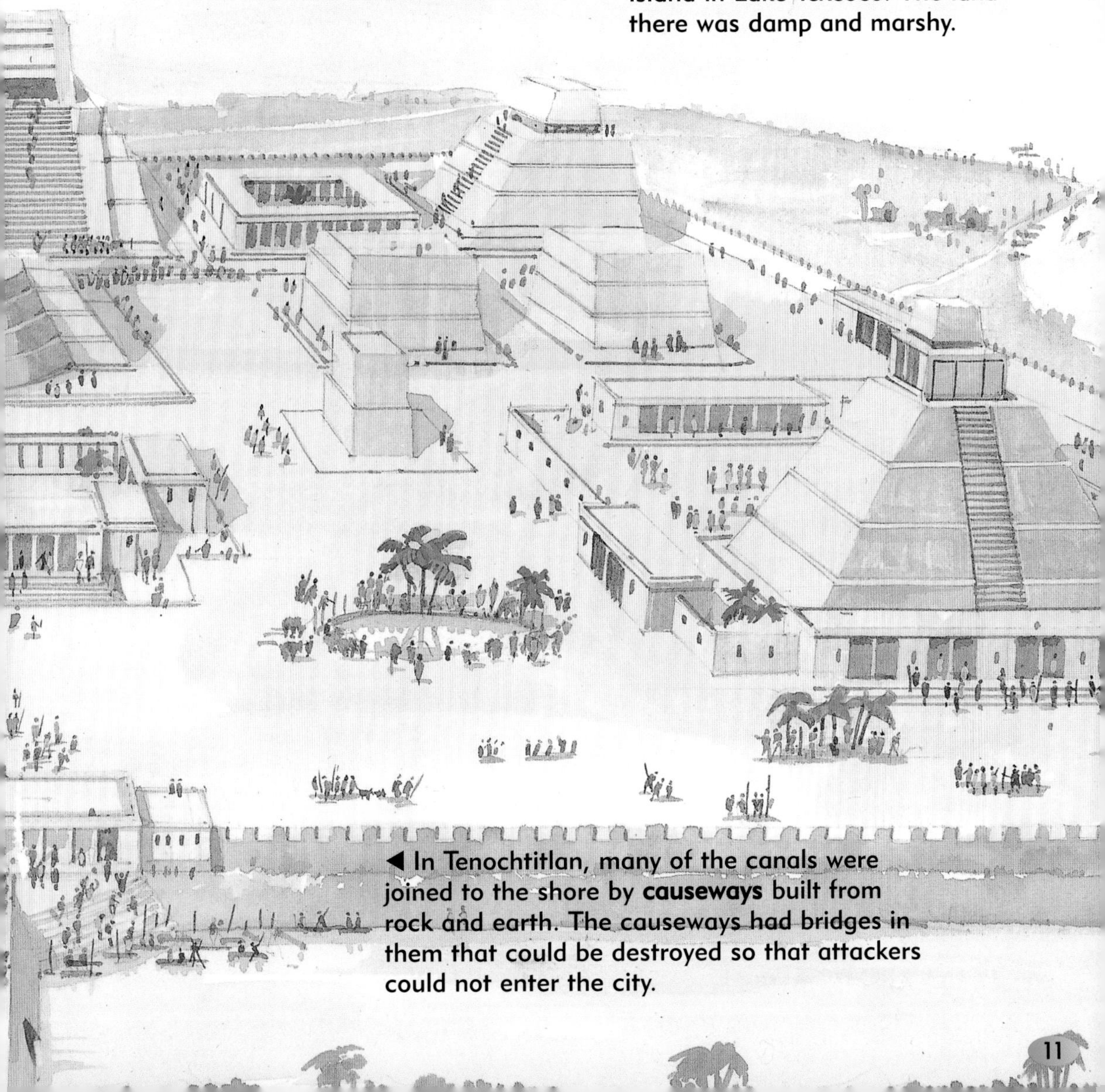

◀ In Tenochtitlan, many of the canals were joined to the shore by **causeways** built from rock and earth. The causeways had bridges in them that could be destroyed so that attackers could not enter the city.

Rulers

The Aztec ruler was known as the huey tlatoani, meaning **great speaker**. He was elected by a council made up of the leaders of the most important Aztec families, or **calpollis**. Advisers helped the great speaker to rule. The most important of these advisers was called the snake woman – even though he was a man!

It was the great speaker's duty to lead the Aztec army into battle. The Aztecs were constantly at war with their neighbors because they needed prisoners to sacrifice to the gods. The lands that were conquered were expected to pay a **tribute** to the Aztecs.

DISK LINK
Would you like to meet an Aztec leader? Then here's your chance! Take a look at The Great Speaker.

▼ This carved stone box shows a great speaker.

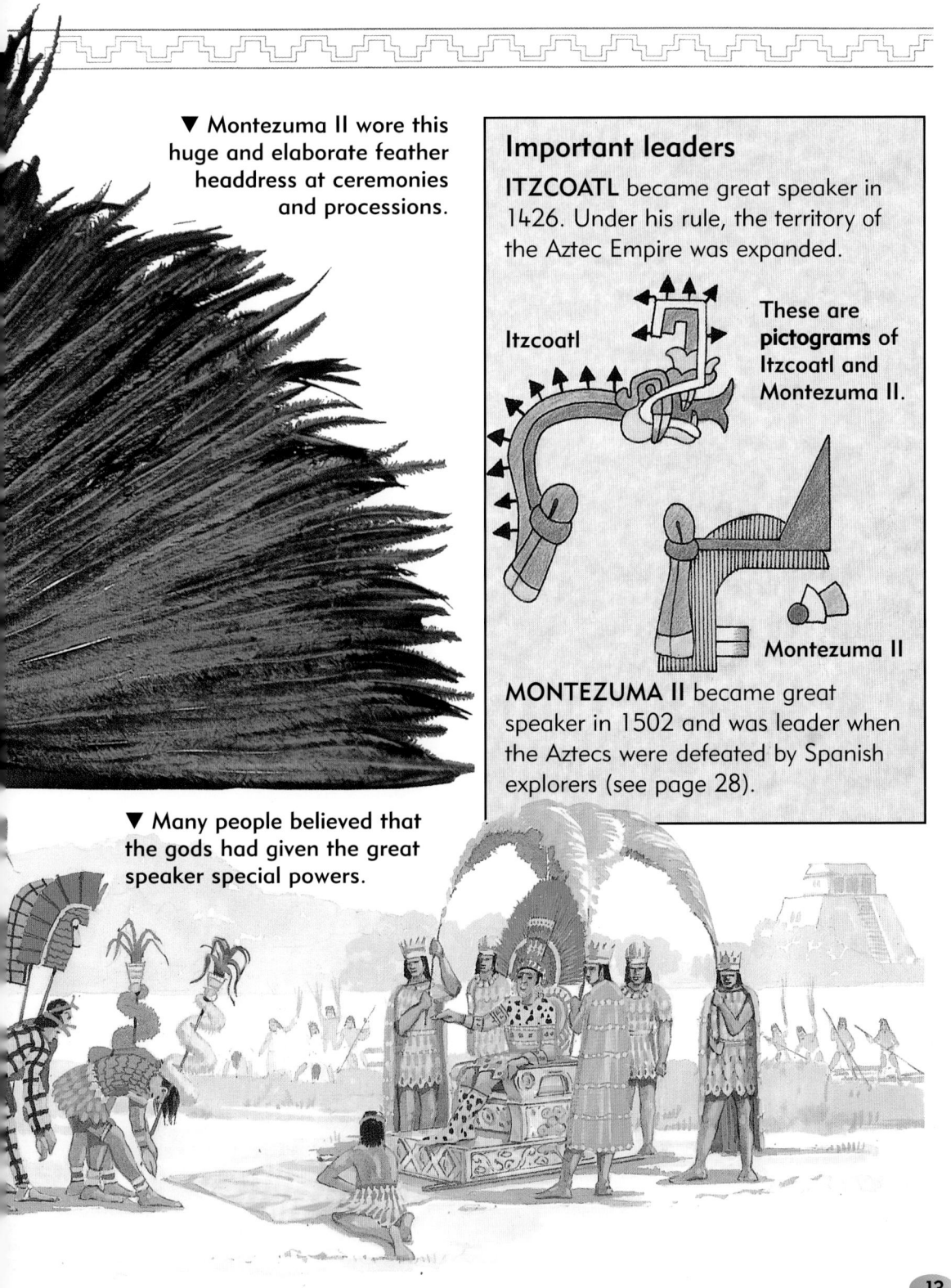

▼ Montezuma II wore this huge and elaborate feather headdress at ceremonies and processions.

Important leaders

ITZCOATL became great speaker in 1426. Under his rule, the territory of the Aztec Empire was expanded.

Itzcoatl

These are **pictograms** of Itzcoatl and Montezuma II.

Montezuma II

MONTEZUMA II became great speaker in 1502 and was leader when the Aztecs were defeated by Spanish explorers (see page 28).

▼ Many people believed that the gods had given the great speaker special powers.

Religion

Religion influenced every part of Aztec life. There were gods for different parts of the natural world and for human activities. The Aztecs believed that the gods decided their fate and that priests could predict future events. The gods were linked by a complicated set of **myths** and legends.

The Aztecs developed different types of calendars. The religious calendar had 260 days in a year. They also had a solar calendar that had 365 days in a year, just like ours. The solar year had 18 months, each with 20 days, plus 5 extra days.

The fifth sun

The Aztecs believed that they lived in the time of the fifth sun. According to Aztec legend, four earlier suns had been destroyed. The first was destroyed by jaguars, the second by hurricanes, the third by fire, and the fourth by floods. They believed that the fifth sun would be destroyed by a huge earthquake.

▶ This is the Aztec calendar stone. At the center is the sun god, Tonatiuh. He is surrounded by symbols of the five world creations. The stone also shows the symbols of the 20 days of the solar month.

◀ This statue is of Coatlicue, the goddess of the earth.

Important gods

HUITZILOPOCHTLI was the god of war and the protector of the Aztecs. The Aztecs fought a special war, called the War of the Flowers, to capture victims to sacrifice to him.

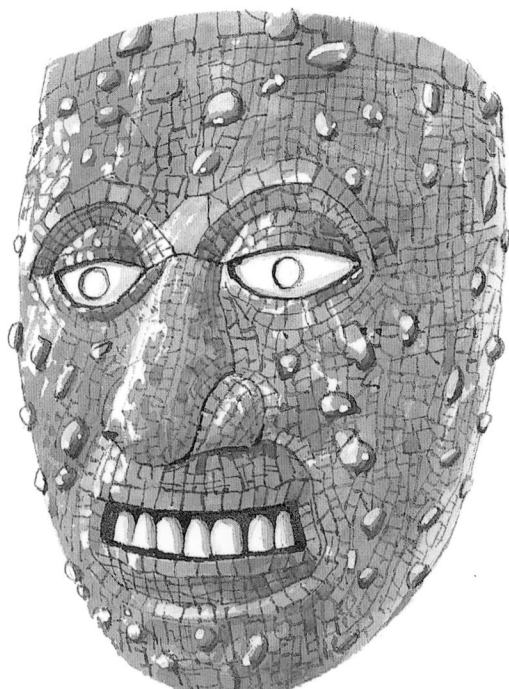

▲ A mask of Quetzalcóatl

QUETZALCÓATL was the god of learning and the arts. His name means *feathered serpent*. The original Quetzalcóatl was probably a leader of the Toltec people, who ruled ancient Mexico long before the Aztecs. According to Aztec legend, Quetzalcóatl would return one day to decide the fate of the Aztecs.

Temples

The Aztecs built large **pyramids** to worship their gods. At the top of each one was a shrine where priests held ceremonies and made sacrifices.

Priests were highly thought of by the Aztecs. They studied the stars and tried to predict the future. Priests were the only people who went out after dark – everybody else was scared of evil spirits.

Near the temples were **tlachtli** courts where the sacred ball game, ulama, was played.

DISK LINK
Would you like to try the sacred ball game? Take the Tlachtli Challenge!

▲ The Aztecs performed hundreds of human sacrifices every year.

◄ The Aztec pyramids had many steps, leading up to a shrine to the gods.

▼ Sharp stone knives, such as this one, were used in the sacrifices.

Sacrifices

Human sacrifices were an important part of Aztec religion. The Aztecs believed that human hearts and blood kept their gods strong and powerful, and that the gods would protect the people and make their crops grow. The Aztecs also believed that if a brave warrior was sacrificed, his strength would be passed on to other warriors. At some ceremonies, Aztec people were sacrificed, but most of the victims were prisoners of war.

Every morning, people made a small sacrifice by pricking their finger or earlobe with a cactus spine and letting a drop of blood fall to the ground.

Farming

Farming was essential to the Aztec way of life. Corn was the most important crop, but the Aztecs also grew avocados, beans, chile peppers, and tomatoes. Each farmer gave the great speaker some of his crops to be stored away in case there was a famine.

There were two types of farmland. Some Aztec farmers cleared a small part of the land or forest by burning the vegetation. Then they planted crops in the fertile ashes. After a few years, when the land became less fertile, they would clear another area.

Around Tenochtitlan, the Aztecs dug up fertile mud from the lake bottom and heaped it on top of woven plant material to make little islands. The islands were called **chinampas**, or floating gardens.

▶ Sometimes, Aztecs planted trees to anchor the chinampas to the bottom of the lake.

▼ A simple **digging stick** was used to prepare the land for planting crops.

DISK LINK
Check out the chinampas when you venture forth in the Aztec Explorer.

Aztec crops

avocado

chile peppers

tomato

corn

beans

Food

Hunting provided much of the meat in the Aztecs' diet. Aztec hunters killed deer, ducks, rabbits, and geese. They raised dogs and turkeys for food and ate lots of vegetables, such as corn, beans, and peppers. They ate a corn tortilla called a **tlaxcalli** with most meals.

DISK LINK
Feast your eyes on an Aztec marketplace in For Sale.

Food facts
● The Aztecs made a chocolate drink from **cacao** beans. They considered it a luxury because they also used cacao beans as money!
● They brewed an alcoholic drink called **octli** from a type of cactus.
● The Aztecs ate fish, turkeys, wild rabbits, and even dogs.

▼ The Aztecs served their food in pottery bowls and often ate using their fingers.

Make your own tlaxcallis

Ingredients:
2 cups corn flour (masa)
1 tsp salt
1 cup (225 ml) cold water

 **1.** Mix the ingredients together.

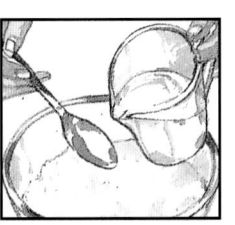 **2.** Gradually add the water to make a soft dough. If the dough is too stiff, add more water.

 **3.** Divide the dough into 12 balls. On waxed paper, roll the balls out into flat, thin circles.

 **4.** Ask an adult to help you fry them in a hot, dry skillet for one minute per side.

Serve your tlaxcallis warm. Fill them with chiles, avocado, beans, tomato, and lettuce and roll them up. Enjoy!

At home

Most Aztecs lived in small, one-room houses. They were made from adobe or from branches or reeds plastered with clay. Only wealthy people could afford large houses. Those houses were often built on raised platforms and had walls made of adobe or stone. The houses had several rooms that opened onto an inner courtyard.

Instead of a bathroom, many houses had a separate sweat room. It was made from stone and was heated by fires built around the outside walls. Inside, the people splashed water onto the hot walls to make them steam. They would stay inside until they began to sweat, and then they would dash out and plunge into the nearest stream or pool.

◀ A statue of the fire god, Xiuhtecuhtli, was placed in the hearth of every house.

▶ Aztec rooms, such as this one, had little furniture. The Aztecs sat on straw cushions and slept on mats in the corners of the room. Each house had a fireplace, where all the cooking was done. It was also used as a shrine to Xiuhtecuhtli, the fire god.

DISK LINK
What were Aztec families like? What did people do in their spare time? Just ask The Great Speaker!

23

Language

The Aztecs spoke a language called Náhuatl. They did not write words made up of letters. Instead, they drew **pictograms,** or pictures that stand for ideas or things. They joined pictograms to form sentences and used them to write down stories and keep records. Aztec manuscripts, called **codices,** were made of folded animal skins or bark paper.

▼ Many Aztec children went to schools that were run by their calpollis, or family groups. They learned about religion, music, and dancing. Boys also learned the skills that they needed to become warriors or tradesmen. Children from noble families went to a temple school, where boys were taught to become priests and girls learned to be temple assistants or midwives.

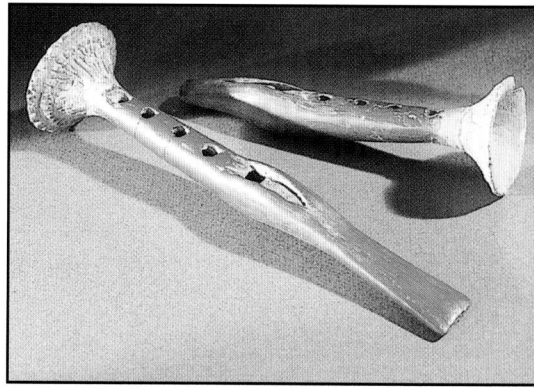

▲ The Aztecs played a variety of musical instruments, such as these flutes. Music was an important part of festivals and religious ceremonies.

▶ This Aztec codex shows offerings being made to the sun god at the top and the god of darkness at the bottom.

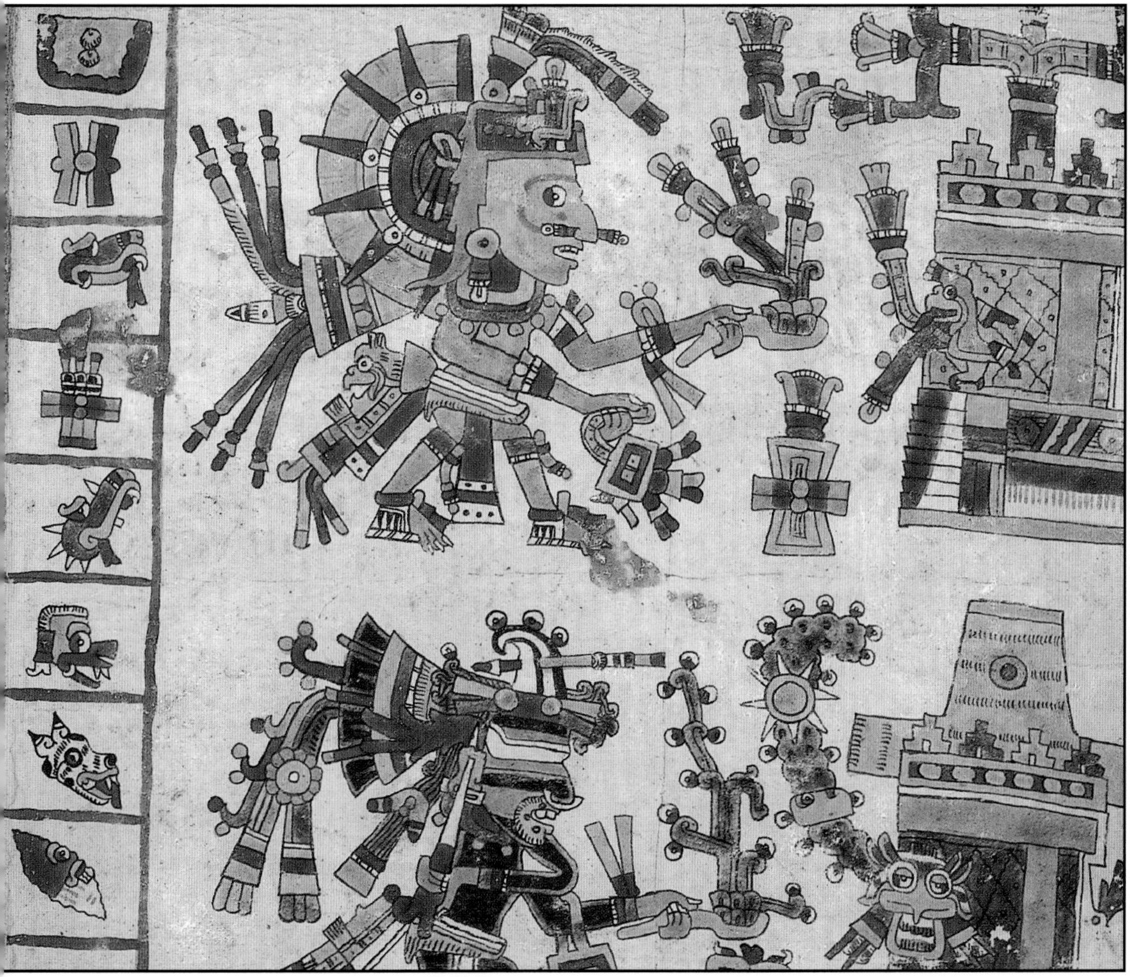

Common pictograms

Just like handwriting today, pictograms varied according to the person who drew them. Are any of these pictograms in the codex above?

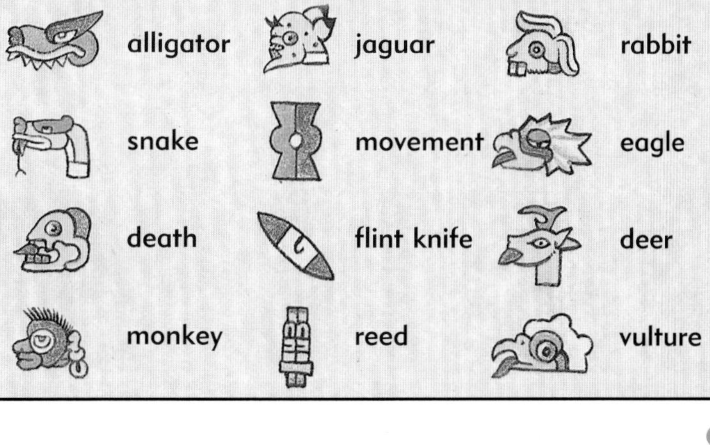

 alligator

 jaguar

 rabbit

 snake

 movement

 eagle

 death

 flint knife

 deer

 monkey

 reed

 vulture

Crafts

In Aztec times, a person's wealth was judged by the beauty of his possessions. A rich man could afford to have a skilled craftsman make the things he needed. Craftsmen were paid in food or other goods.

The Aztecs did not use metal for tools or weapons. They did not have iron or any other strong metal. Gold and copper were used to make delicate statues and jewelry.

▲ Some Aztecs wore a golden ornament, such as this one, through their lips.

The Aztecs made fine pots decorated in gold. They did not have pottery wheels, so they made pots by building up coils of clay and smoothing them out.

The volcanic rock found in Mexico is very soft, and it could easily be carved with the stone tools the Aztecs used. The people made detailed stone carvings and statues from stone.

Aztecs trimmed brightly colored feathers and bound them together to make clothes and headdresses. They also used feathers to decorate warriors' shields and weapons

▼ This shield was made from feathers.

A type of volcanic stone called **obsidian** was used to make vases, mirrors, and blades for knives.

▼ Mirrors, such as this one, were made from polished obsidian.

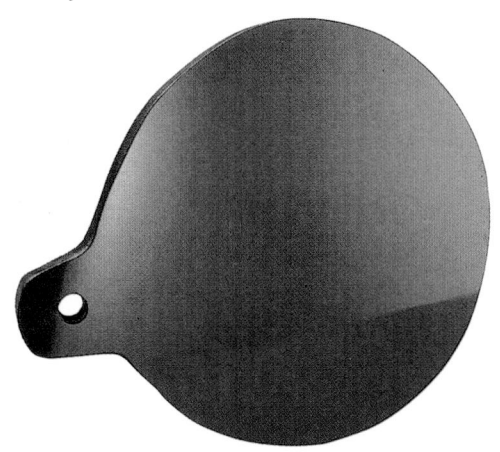

Clothes

Aztec clothes reflected a person's age and position in society. Most clothes were made from the fiber of a cactus called the **maguey** plant. Only the rich could afford to wear cotton. Their garments were brightly colored and covered with beautiful embroidery. Warriors wore ornate feather headdresses, and the most important warriors were allowed to wear costumes that made them look like jaguars or eagles. Men wore a loincloth, called a **maxtlatl**, with a cape over one shoulder. Women wore a loose tunic over a skirt tied with a belt.

Both men and women wore emerald, jade, and opal jewelry. They also wore lots of bright, multicolored makeup.

DISK LINK
Stay on the lookout for clues that will help you through the Survival Adventure.

Invasion!

Aztec civilization was at its peak when Montezuma II was great speaker. At this time the Spanish were looking for new lands to conquer. In 1519, a Spaniard named Hernando Cortés arrived in Mexico with an army of about 300 men.

At first, the Aztecs believed that Cortés was the god Quetzalcóatl, returning to decide their fate as the priests had foretold. They did not know whether to welcome him or be wary of him.

Within two years, the Spanish had killed most of the Aztec people and destroyed the city of Tenochtitlan. The Aztecs were no match against the Spanish with their cannons and armor.

▼ Aztec myths predicted that when Quetzalcóatl returned, he would have a pale face and a dark beard. To the Aztecs, Cortés, with his pale skin and dark beard, looked just like the god.

DISK LINK
Step back in time to find out more about the Spanish invasion in Time Warp.

Food for the people

The Aztecs told many stories about their gods and about the world around them. Often these stories would attempt to explain something that the people did not really understand. This is a story about the discovery of corn.

The gods found that creating people was much more difficult than creating the rest of the world! They had attempted to make people many times, but each attempt had failed. Finally, they created some creatures that seemed to be just about right. There was only one problem. The people that they had made did not seem to know what to eat, or even how to eat. The people were starving, but the gods couldn't figure out what to do about it. All the other animals they had created knew exactly how to feed themselves without any help.

The gods worried as they watched the people growing thinner. Every day, they tried to think of different ways to help the people find the food that they needed.

One day, some ants came to the place where the gods were discussing what to do about the starving people.

"We know where there is food," said one of the ants. "We will carry it here for you to give to the new people."

"Great!" said Quetzalcóatl, the god who was most worried about the people. "But why don't you just tell us where the food is, and we will tell the people?"

"No, no, no!" said the ants. "We can't possibly do that. It's our secret."

The ants wanted the gods to look favorably upon them. They also thought that the people might be useful to them in the future. This is why they wanted to help the gods by supplying the people with food.

The next day, the ants carried food to the gods. This food was very small and hard. In fact, the pieces were so tiny that each of the ants could easily carry one grain. The gods had never seen anything like it! They chewed the hard grains until they were soft, and then they placed them on the lips of the people. The people swallowed the grains and soon began to look and feel much better.

The ants continued to carry the food to the gods every day, but they would not tell them where it came from. The gods had to wait patiently for the ants to bring the grains. Then they would chew it for the people and place it on their lips.

As much as Quetzalcóatl loved the people, he became tired of feeding them. All the gods were falling behind in their responsibilities. While they were chewing the food for the people, they could not concentrate on making the sun shine, or the rain fall, or the rivers flow. Each day, when the ants arrived with the grains, the gods sighed deeply and grew more and more irritated.

One day, Quetzalcóatl decided to find out for himself where the food was. He turned himself into a black ant and waited for the ants to pass by. As the ants marched past, he slipped into line and marched with them. The procession led to the foot of a tall mountain, then disappeared through a tiny crack in the rock. Inside the mountain, there was an enormous cavern, and Quetzalcóatl saw a huge pile of food. Copying the other ants, he picked up a grain and stepped back into the line.

When the procession of ants reached the gods, Quetzalcóatl returned to his own form. "You could not keep the secret of the food from me!" he said to the ants.

"But you need us to help you!" said one of the ants. "The people are much too big to fit in through the tiny crack in the side of the mountain."

Quetzalcóatl turned to the thunder god and whispered in his ear. The thunder god stood up and raised his hand. All of the ants scuttled away in fear.

A flash of lightning struck the mountain, causing a huge crack. The grains of food spilled out over the ground. The people ran to see what had happened.

One of the people picked up a grain and put it in his mouth. The others copied him and ate their fill of food.

But there were many grains left over. Quetzalcóatl showed the people how to plant the grains, so that more food would grow on new plants. These plants grew into the food we now call corn.

The gods were happy to know that the people could feed themselves. And the people were happy because they now knew what to eat and how to grow it.

As for the ants, they found that the people could still be useful. The people began to find other new and delicious foods that the ants could also share!

How we know

How do we know about the Aztecs, even though they lived such a long time ago?

Evidence from the ground
The Spanish invaders demolished most of Tenochtitlan, destroying a lot of the evidence of the Aztec way of life. However, some Aztec artifacts remain, and the ruins of a few temples that were not destroyed still stand today.

▲ This temple was built in about A.D. 250, at Teotihuacán, in the Valley of Mexico. It is one of the few temples that still stands today.

▲ Some Aztec codices have survived.

Evidence from books
The Spanish destroyed most of the Aztecs' codices, although a few have survived. One Spaniard, Bernardino de Sahagun, translated some Aztec codices soon after the conquest. Other members of the Spanish invading forces wrote accounts of Aztec life as it was when they arrived.

Evidence around us
Today, descendants of the Aztecs still live in Mexico, and some of their customs date back to Aztec times. Many speak a form of the Aztec language, Náhuatl, and some of the words have passed into other languages, such as *tomatl* (tomato), *chocolatl* (chocolate), and *ahuacatl* (avocado).

Glossary

Anahuac The name that the Aztecs gave to the lands of their empire in Mexico.

cacao A bean used to make chocolate and cocoa.

calpolli A group made up of closely related Aztec people. Each calpolli had a head man who made decisions for the group.

causeway A type of road built to cross water.

chinampas Small island farms built by the Aztecs.

codices A type of ancient manuscript. Aztec codices were written on animal skins or bark paper and folded to make a book.

digging stick A simple, long, straight stick used to dig and plow the earth.

empire A large area of conquered lands, including many different towns.

great speaker The leader of the Aztec Empire.

maguey A plant belonging to the cactus family.

maxtlatl A cloth wrapped and tied around the hips, worn by Aztec men.

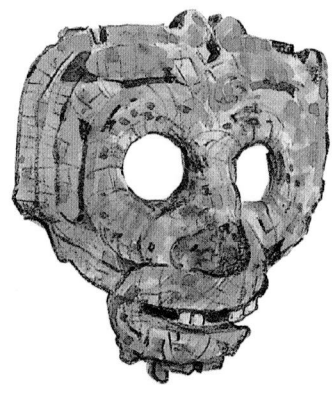

myths Traditional stories about gods or heroes. Myths are sometimes based on the truth, and they explain how people think about the world.

obsidian A dark, glassy rock.

octli An alcoholic drink made from the sap of the maguey plant.

pictogram A symbol that represents a thing, an idea, or a word.

plateau A large area of high, flat land.

pyramids Buildings with a square base and sloping sides. The Aztecs built pyramids as temples to worship their gods.

sacrifice Killing an animal or a person as an offering to the gods.

tlachtli The court where the sacred Aztec ball game, ulama, was played. Two teams tried to pass a ball through a hoop using their elbows, hips, and knees.

tlaxcalli An Aztec word for corn flatbread. They are still eaten today, but they are usually known by the Spanish word *tortilla*.

tribute A form of tax paid to the Aztec ruler by the people living in the towns throughout the Aztec Empire.

Lab pages

Photocopy these sheets and use them to make your own notes.

Rules of patolli

Patolli was one of the Aztecs' favorite games. Now you can play it on your computer. The rules are easy to learn. It is a two-player game, so you'll need someone to play against.

- Each player starts off with 10 jade pebbles and six game pieces. To win, you must either get all your pieces around the board or win all of your opponent's pebbles.

- Before the game begins, both players must agree how many pebbles they are going to gamble. You must each bet the same number of pebbles.

- Players take turns throwing five cacao beans. Each bean has a dot on it.

- If one dot lands face up, you can move one square, or move a piece onto the board for the first time.

- If two dots land face up, you can move two squares.

- If three dots land face up, you can move three squares.

- If four dots land face up, you can move four squares.

- But if five dots land face up, you can move TEN squares!

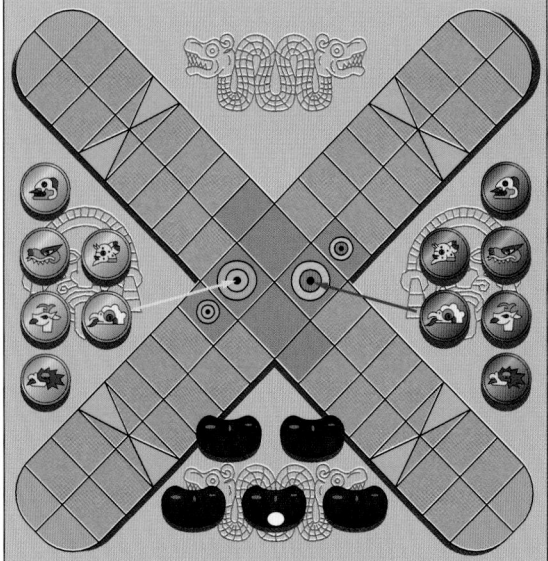

▲ The pieces begin their journey around the board from the start squares. But before you can move a piece onto the board, you must throw a one with the beans.

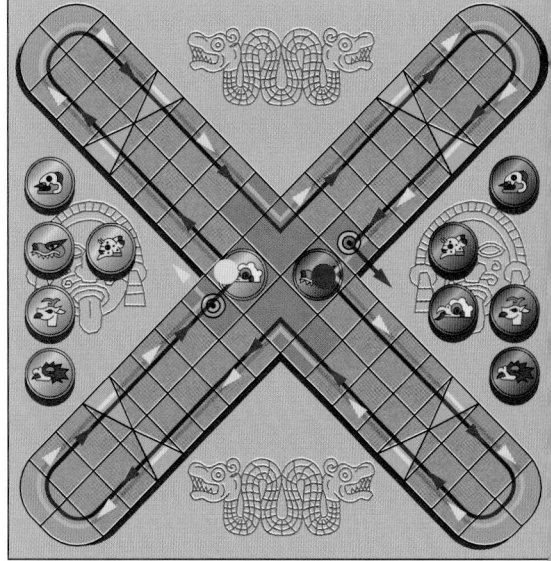

▲ The pieces move in a clockwise direction until they reach the finish squares. Each player has his or her own finish square.

- When a piece lands on a finish square, it is taken off the board. Every time you get a piece off the board, your opponent must give you a jade pebble.

- The first player to get all his or her pieces off the board is the winner.

- If you lose all your pieces during play, your opponent automatically wins the game.

- You must move one of your pieces if you possibly can – you are not allowed to skip your turn.

- You may move only one piece at a time – you are not allowed to split your throw between different pieces.

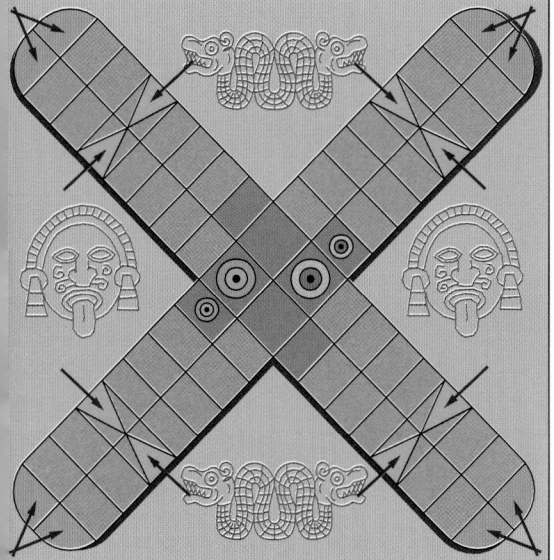

▲ Watch out for the eight squares marked with a triangle. If one of your pieces lands on one of these squares, you must give your opponent two of your jade pebbles.

On the other hand, the two squares at each of the four ends of the board are good luck. Whenever one of your pieces lands on one of these squares, you get another turn and can throw the beans again. Hooray!

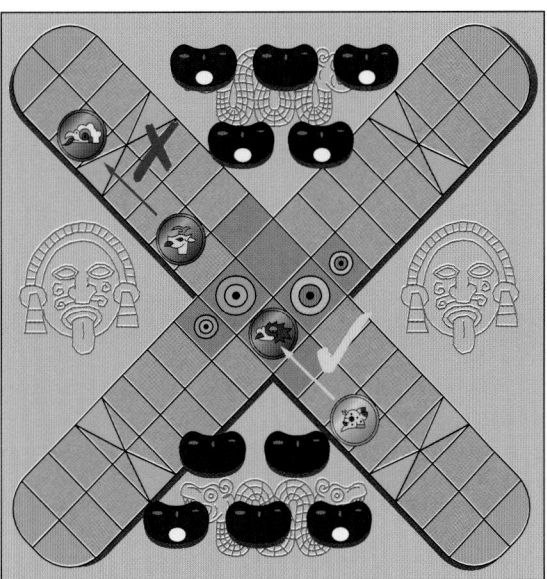

▲ You may not land on a square occupied by one of your own pieces.

You are also not allowed on a square that is taken by one of your opponent's pieces – unless it is on one of the eight purple squares in the middle of the board!

If you land on one of your opponent's pieces in one of these squares, the opponent's piece is taken off the board, and he or she must start all over again.

Loading your INTERFACT disk

INTERFACT is easy to load. But, before you begin, quickly run through the checklist on the opposite page to ensure that your computer is ready to run the program.

Your INTERFACT CD-ROM will run on both PCs with Windows and on Apple Macs. To make sure that your computer meets the system requirements, check the list below.

SYSTEM REQUIREMENTS

PC/WINDOWS
- Pentium 100Mhz processor
- Windows 95 or 98 (or later)
- 16Mb RAM (24Mb recommended for Windows 98)
- VGA 256 color monitor
- SoundBlaster-compatible soundcard
- 1Mb graphics card
- Double-speed CD-ROM drive

APPLE MAC
- 68020 processor (PowerMac or G3/iMac recommended)
- System 7.0 (or later)
- 16Mb RAM
- Color monitor set to at least 480 x 640 pixels and 256 colors
- Double-speed CD-ROM drive

LOADING INSTRUCTIONS

You can run INTERFACT from the CD – you don't need to install it on your hard drive.

PC WITH WINDOWS 95 OR 98

The program should start automatically when you put the disk in the CD drive. If it does not, follow these instructions.

1. Put the disk in the CD drive
2. Open MY COMPUTER
3. Double-click on the CD drive icon
4. Double-click on the icon called AZTECS

PC WITH WINDOWS 3.1 OR 3.11

1. Put the disk in the CD drive
2. Select RUN from the FILE menu in the PROGRAM MANAGER
3. Type D:\AZTECS (Where D is the letter of your CD drive)
4. Press the RETURN key

APPLE MAC

1. Put the disk in the CD drive
2. Double-click on the INTERFACT icon
3. Double-click on the icon called AZTECS

CHECKLIST

● Firstly, make sure that your computer and monitor meet the system requirements as set out on page 40.

● Ensure that your computer, monitor and CD-ROM drive are all switched on and working normally.

● It is important that you do not have any other applications, such as wordprocessors, running. Before starting INTERFACT quit all other applications.

● Make sure that any screen savers have been switched off.

● If you are running INTERFACT on a PC with Windows 3.1 or 3.11, make sure that you type in the correct instructions when loading the disk, using a colon (:) not a semi-colon (;) and a back slash (\) not a forward slash (/). Also, do not use any other punctuation or put any spaces between letters.

How to use INTERFACT

INTERFACT is easy to use.
First find out how to load the program
(see page 40), then read these simple
instructions and dive in!

You will find that there are lots of different features to explore.
To select one, operate the controls on the right-hand side of the screen. You will see that the main area of the screen changes as you click on different features.

For example, this is what your screen will look like in For Sale, a scene from the ancient Aztec marketplace at Tlatelolco that you can explore. Once you've selected a feature, just click on the main screen to start playing.

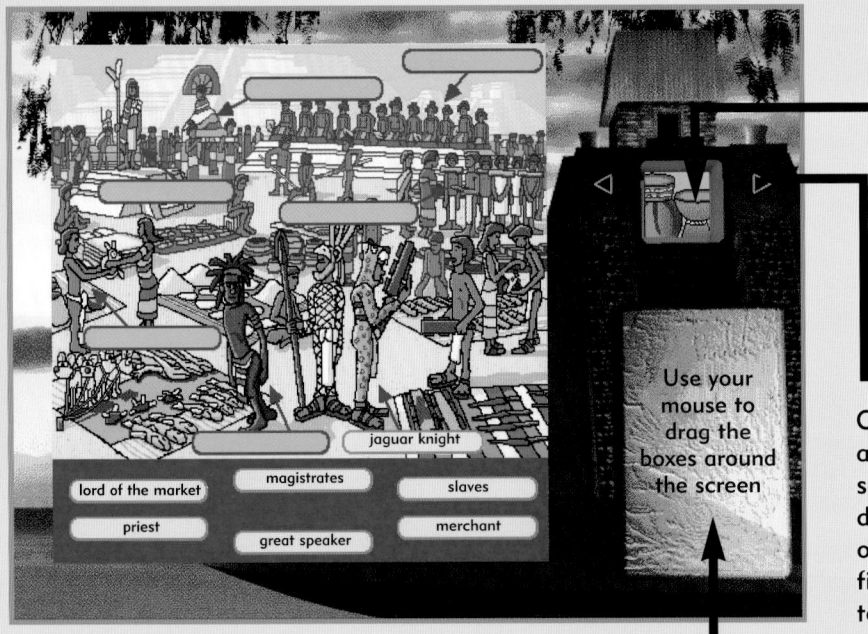

Click here to select the feature you want to play.

Use your mouse to drag the boxes around the screen

jaguar knight

lord of the market

magistrates

slaves

priest

great speaker

merchant

Click on the arrow keys to scroll through the different features on the disk or find your way to the exit.

This is the text box, where instructions and directions appear. See page 4 to find out what's on the disk.

DISK LINKS

When you read the book, you'll come across Disk Links. These show you where to find activities on the disk that relate to the page you are reading. Use the arrow keys to find the icon on screen that matches the one in the Disk Link.

DISK LINK
Put your Aztec know-how to the test when you take the Tlachtli Challenge!

BOOKMARKS

As you explore the features on the disk, you'll bump into Bookmarks. These show you where to look in the book for more information about the topic on screen. Just turn to the page of the book shown in the Bookmark.

23

LAB PAGES

On pages 36 and 37, you'll find pages to photocopy. These are for making notes and recording any thoughts or ideas you may have as you read the book.

HOT DISK TIPS

• After you have chosen the feature you want to play, remember to move the cursor from the icon to the main screen before clicking the mouse again.

• If you don't know how to use one of the on-screen controls, simply touch it with your cursor. An explanation will pop up in the text box!

• Keep a close eye on the cursor. When it changes from an arrow ➔ to a hand, 👉 click your mouse and something will happen.

• Any words that appear on screen in blue and underlined are "hot." This means you can touch them with the cursor for more information.

• Explore the screen! There are secret hot spots and hidden surprises to find.

Troubleshooting

If you have a problem with your INTERFACT disk, you should find the solution here. If you still have a problem, send us an email at helpline@two-canpublishing.com.

QUICK FIXES Run through these general checkpoints before consulting COMMON PROBLEMS (see opposite page).

QUICK FIXES PC WITH WINDOWS 3.1 OR 3.11

1 Check that you have the minimum system requirements: 386/33Mhz, VGA color monitor, 4Mb of RAM.

2 Make sure you have typed in the correct instructions: a colon (:) not a semi-colon (;) and a back slash (\) not a forward slash (/). Also, do not put any spaces between letters or punctuation.

3 It is important that you do not have any other programs running. Before you start **INTERFACT**, hold down the Control key and press Escape. If you find that other programs are open, click on them with the mouse, then click the End Task key.

QUICK FIXES PC WITH WINDOWS 95

1 Make sure you have typed in the correct instructions: a colon (:) not a semi-colon (;) and a back slash(\) not a forward slash (/). Also, do not put any spaces between letters or punctuation.

2 It is important that you do not have any other programs running. Before you start **INTERFACT**, look at the task bar. If you find that other programs are open, click with the right mouse button and select Close from the pop-up menu.

MACINTOSH

1 Make sure that you have the minimum system requirements: 68020 processor, 640x480 color display, system 7.0 (or a later version), and 4Mb of RAM.

2 It is important that you do not have any other programs running. Before you start **INTERFACT**, click on the application menu in the top right-hand corner. Select each of the open applications and select Quit from the File menu.

COMMON PROBLEMS

Symptom: Cannot load disk.
Problem: There is not enough space available on your hard disk.
Solution: Make more space available by deleting old applications and files you don't use until 6Mb of free space is available.

Symptom: Disk will not run.
Problem: There is not enough memory available.
Solution: *Either* quit other open applications (see Quick Fixes) *or* increase your machine's RAM by adjusting the Virtual Memory.

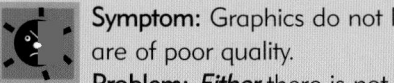
Symptom: Graphics do not load or are of poor quality.
Problem: *Either* there is not enough memory available *or* you have the wrong display setting.
Solution: *Either* quit other applications (see Quick Fixes) *or* make sure that your monitor control is set to 640x480x256 or VGA.

Symptom: There is no sound (PCs only).
Problem: Your sound card is not Soundblaster compatible.
Solution: Try to configure your sound settings to make them Soundblaster compatible (refer to your sound card manual for more details).

Symptom: Your machine freezes.
Problem: There is not enough memory available.
Solution: *Either* quit other applications (see Quick Fixes) *or* increase your machine's RAM by adjusting the Virtual Memory.

Symptom: Text does not fit neatly into boxes, and "hot" copy does not bring up extra information.
Problem: Standard fonts on your computer have been moved or deleted.
Solution: Reinstall standard fonts. The PC version requires Arial; the Macintosh version requires Helvetica. See your computer manual for further information.

Index

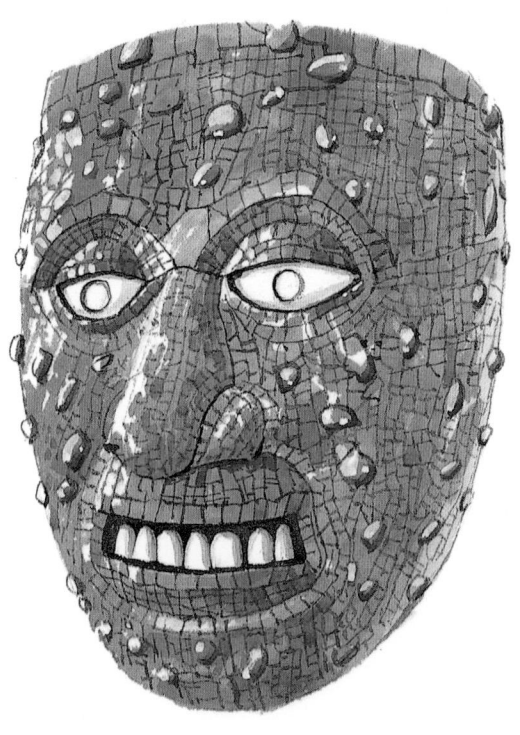